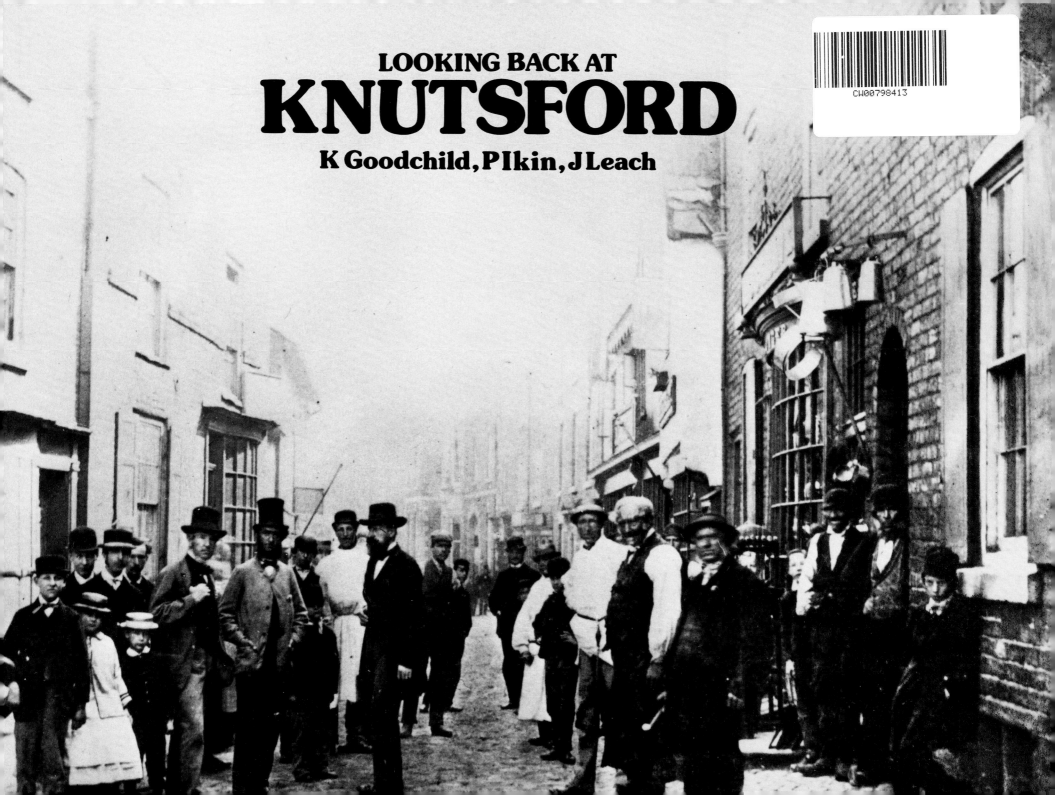

LOOKING BACK AT
KNUTSFORD

K Goodchild, P Ikin, J Leach

Willow Publishing 1984
Willow Cottage, 36 Moss Lane,
Timperley, Altrincham,
Cheshire, WA15 6SZ.

ISBN 0 946361 09 6

Printed by The Commercial
Centre Ltd., Clowes Street,
Hollinwood, Oldham.

Acknowledgements

For years, The Rev. Will Strachan, Chairman of
the Knutsford Historical & Archaeological
Association, has been trying to persuade Mr. Bob
Bowles, to commit to print his unique collection of
photographs of Old Knutsford.

Due to other commitments over the years, this
has not been possible until now, when it has fallen
to his daughter, Pat Ikin, and two local historians,
Joan Leach and Kath Goodchild, to produce this
book.

We hope it will revive happy memories for
older Knutsfordians, and that it will bridge the gap
between then and now, for all newcomers to
Knutsford.

We are indebted to Bob Bowles to Mr. Fred
McDowell, Miss D. Barronian, Mr. Howard
Lawless, Mr. Rod Monnington, Mr. Colin Wright,
and all others who have generously shared their
photographs and reminiscences with us.

March, 1984

Introduction

A 'potted' history of one's town, as an introduction
to a book of photographs, is not the easiest of tasks.

One begins with a name of Scandinavian origin
which has no written record, but a tradition that
associates it with King Canute. It could be that
Canute camped here with his army on his march
to Scotland in 1017.

Other place names around the district have
their origins in earlier Norse and Danish visits –
some we fear, were none too peaceful – Cheshire
was ravaged in 980.

Cunetesford is recorded in the Domesday book
of 1086 – 'it was and is waste'. Had the people
been murdered, or had they fled the onslaught of
the rampaging Normans in 1070? We don't know
– there are no records to tell us except 'it was and
is waste'.

Gradually it was deemed safe to return and
settle on ground near the Lily Brook (King Street,
Nether Knutsford), and up the hill (Chelford
Road, Over Knutsford).

From these beginnings Knutsford was
established as a Market Town in 1292 with a
Charter for a market on Saturdays, and a fair held
annually in June. A later Charter in 1332 gave the
right to hold a second fair in October. At this time
Richard Massey of Tatton and William de Tabley
held the Manorial rights divided between them.

In 1300, Peter Legh purchased the estate of
Norbury Booths from William de Tabley, and the
Leghs came on the scene as feudal Lords of
Knutsford. As troubled times became more
peaceful the Leghs of Norbury Booths became the
'squires' of Knutsford, owning much property,
choosing the master for the Grammar School,
paying the preaching minister, and worshipping
with the townsfolk in the parochial chapel. The
Egertons of Tatton became involved in local affairs
around 1700.

The tradesmen prospered. Knutsford considered itself to be the capital of mid-Cheshire, coming fourth in size after Chester, Stockport and Congleton.

The Quarter Sessions were held here from the 16th century, and in 1817 the House of Correction, later the County Gaol, was built. A large workhouse (now Cranford Lodge Hospital) was run jointly with Altrincham. The old administrative area known as the Bucklow Hundred, included Altrincham. The several inns were always well patronised by travellers passing through as Knutsford was on the main road to London. The townsfolk saw the Royalists and the Roundheads camped at different times on Knutsford Heath. No doubt there was the odd debt, but we believe the traders would do nicely out of the two opposing armies.

Lord Torrington wrote of Knutsford in 1790 'a clean well built, well placed town where the cotton trade brings plenty'. But no Industrial Revolution came to trouble Knutsford. There was no huge expansion of population, no ugly mills belching dirt and eating coal. Instead Knutsford had a cottage industry, silk button making, and flax, silk and cotton were woven on hand looms. Some worked in communal lofts above the living accommodation of the cottages.

The gentry of Cheshire and Lancashire came to Knutsford in the 18th and 19th centuries for the races on the Heath, and the Assemblies at the 'George'.

Mrs. Gaskell's memories of a happy childhood put 'Cranford', alias Knutsford, on the literary map forever. She described Knutsford when she wrote of Duncombe in Mr. Harrison's Confessions 'a very picturesque place. The houses are anything but regular, they may be mean in their details, but altogether they look well; they have not that unrelieved front which many towns of far more pretensions present. Here and there a bow window – every now and then a gable, cutting up against the sky – occasionally a projecting upper storey throws good effect of light and shadow along the street'.

Knutsford was looked on kindly by many others who knew the town. C. E. Montague wrote in the 1920s 'For warmth give me red Knutsford: it glows like a firelit room of old masters in heavy gilt frames; its mellow, settled habitableness the sum of all that men and women neither poor nor very rich could think of, in about nine hundred years, to make their town good to live in'. But there was the odd 'blot' on the landscape – there were some squalid houses, there were the poor, there was the odd scandal, but, overriding all, is a picture of life in a small, friendly town.

(Right) The George

(Below)
The May Day procession passing the White Bear Inn in the early 1930s, before the houses alongside it were demolished to make way for King Edward Road.

In the 1860s, Canute Place was used for a livestock and farm produce market, which was later transferred to the 'George' Yard. The small heath was known as Market Green, and Canute Place was known as Heathside.

The square served as a bus station in the 1930s, until the present Stanley Park Bus and Coach Station was built on the site of the old gaol.

The White Bear Inn was probably a 17th Century inn, but we have not found any written evidence for it before the Land Tax Assessment names Joseph Preston as the licensee in 1780. In the 1600s, the licences for inns were granted to the licensee in his name, and the name of his inn is not recorded. Occasionally, inn and licensee are named in other documents to fill in this gap, but not in the case of the White Bear. The White Bear, although smaller than Knutsford's other coaching inns was well positioned to catch the trade of travellers passing through Knutsford, and to provide liquid refreshment for those grown thirsty cheering on their favourite horse at race days on the Heath.

Pigots directory for 1829 notes that 'the Aurora (horsedrawn coach) calls at the White Bear, Heathside every evening at half-past eight, and goes through Newcastle and Birmingham' to London. On the return journey it called at five o'clock on the way to Liverpool.

Later, services ran to Northwich and Manchester, and in 1855 an omnibus (horse-drawn) left every morning at 8.15 and every afternoon at 3.45 for Bowdon Station to connect with the trains to and from Manchester. This was in the days before the railway came to Knutsford.

4

A peaceful view of Tatton Street, when compared with today's busy street. In the road, just before Minshull Street, is the public weighing machine, which records show, was here in 1792. The shop next to it is Jackson's Pork Butchers. Driving the pony and trap is 'Coffee Dean', a farmer from Over Tabley Hall Farm, who was known for his teetotalism. There was no cider or beer for his haymakers!

The thatched cottage with the board over the door, was the 'Feathers' Inn for many years, reverting to a cottage again in 1910. A small shop separates it from the 'Lord Eldon' Inn. Augustus Caesar kept this shop. Later, the Caesar family, made rustic summer houses and garden furniture, and these were displayed for sale in the grounds of their cottage, next to the library. The two brothers who had this business were called Henry and Julius. We feel Augustus and Julius, when they were schoolboys, must have been subjected to a lot of ribbing with names like these.

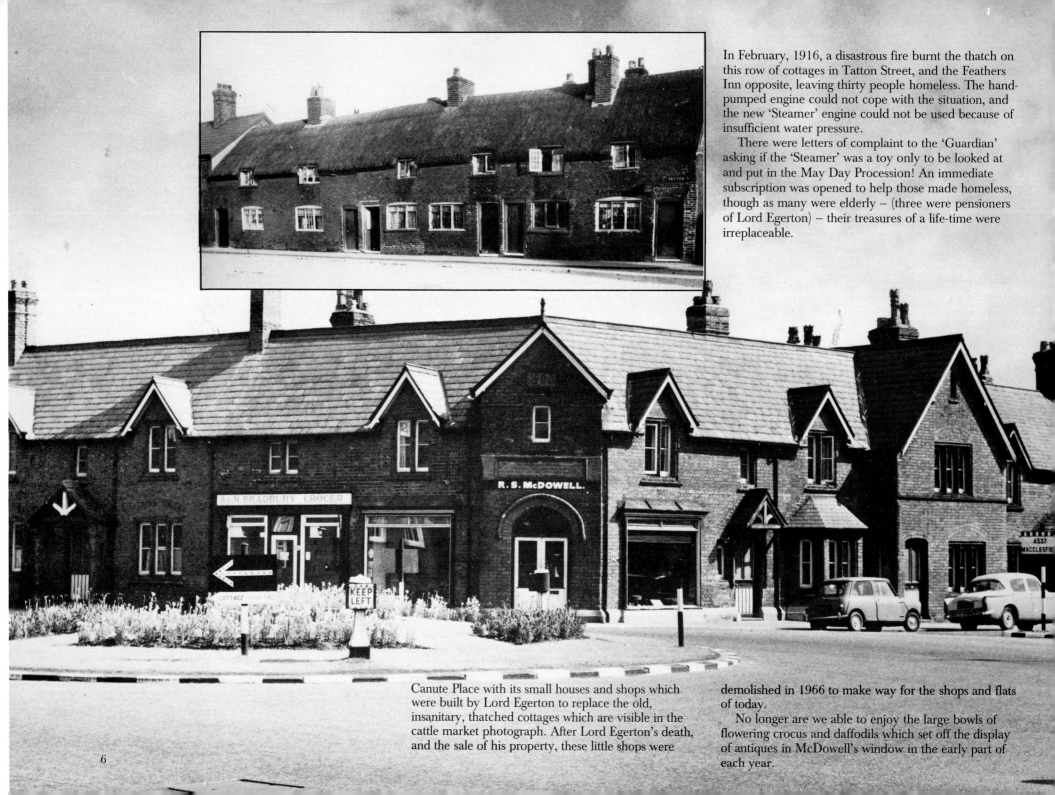

In February, 1916, a disastrous fire burnt the thatch on this row of cottages in Tatton Street, and the Feathers Inn opposite, leaving thirty people homeless. The hand-pumped engine could not cope with the situation, and the new 'Steamer' engine could not be used because of insufficient water pressure.

There were letters of complaint to the 'Guardian' asking if the 'Steamer' was a toy only to be looked at and put in the May Day Procession! An immediate subscription was opened to help those made homeless, though as many were elderly – (three were pensioners of Lord Egerton) – their treasures of a life-time were irreplaceable.

Canute Place with its small houses and shops which were built by Lord Egerton to replace the old, insanitary, thatched cottages which are visible in the cattle market photograph. After Lord Egerton's death, and the sale of his property, these little shops were demolished in 1966 to make way for the shops and flats of today.

No longer are we able to enjoy the large bowls of flowering crocus and daffodils which set off the display of antiques in McDowell's window in the early part of each year.

(Right)

This lamp post was a popular meeting place for boys. Knutsfordian, Harold Tarrant, remembers a time, about 1910, when he and his pals tried without success, to collect 100 car numbers to send to the 'Daily Mail' for a prize.

The building in the background, now part of the Angel Hotel, has had a varied history. It may have been built as a theatre for travelling players, and has also been used by the Y.M.C.A. In this photo it was serving as a warehouse.

(Below)

For many years, the corner of Canute Place opposite the Red Cow Inn, was known as 'Mary Moston's Corner', after the keeper of the stationery shop. Much earlier, the Sessions House had stood at the corner. It was already old, when the Post Chaise (now the Red Cow) was built opposite in 1758. The Post Chaise has been known over the years as the Red Cow or Brown Cow. It took its name from a famous breed of Cheshire cattle. Vegetables for the inn were grown on a plot of land in what is now Stanley Road, near the present day traffic lights.

(Left)
Princess Street in 1865 – still very much a residential street. The two ladies at the open window are the Misses Holland, cousins to Mrs. Gaskell. It was still an event to be photographed, so the local residents willingly posed, before going about their business.

(Below)
Princess Street in the early 1900s. The large Georgian house had been home to several Knutsford doctors, including Richard Dean, Charles Merriman and Theodore Fennell.

Richard Dean's second wife, was Bessie Holland, sister to Mary and Lucy Holland, and cousin to Mrs. Gaskell. She described the house as having four staircases.

Dr. Fennell was living here when the photograph was taken. During the first World War, he declared that conscientious objectors could 'lie in the road' before he would treat them! Mr. Harold Wright remembers the old house being demolished in 1931.

(Above)
The Chemist shop of G. Simpson, Princess Street, made famous as Miss Matty's tea shop in the novel 'Cranford'. In 1835 it was still a private dwelling house owned and occupied by a Miss Harker, when it was advertised for sale in the Macclesfield Courier of 15th October, 1835. Now, alas, a gutted ruin, after a disastrous fire in December, 1983.

(Above Right)
Grice's Bicycle Shop and Garage, Princess Street. Mr. Grice is standing outside his shop, warmly dressed for a drive in his car, which was an Argyle, made about 1903.

(Right)
The first wedding in Knutsford to use motor cars to convey the bridal party, instead of the usual horse-drawn carriages. The date is June 12th 1909, and Miss Nellie Leach is marrying Mr. Clifford J. Billington.

The cars for the wedding were supplied by Jackson Brothers of Princess Street. Billington's shop stood on Princess Street, after the Red Cow.

This photo of the Town Hall, built by Lord Egerton in 1871–2, must have been taken from the roof of the Sessions House. It was designed by Alfred Waterhouse, the eminent Victorian architect. Manchester Town Hall, and the Natural History Museum at Kensington are two of the better known examples of his work.

The ground floor was a market hall where dairy produce was sold. The archways were open, so it must have been very draughty for the stallholders. Above it was a meeting hall. A concert held here in 1883 had a programme which included readings, songs, duets and a selection from the repertoire of Cross Town Brass Band. Tickets for this concert cost 3d. (better seats) or 1d.

Perhaps, because it had no facilities for the Town Council, it was not used as much as had been intended. In the 1950s and 60s, it was occupied by the Boys' Club. It is now a furniture showroom.

A view of the prison taken from the tower of the Parish Church opposite. Knutsford gaol was built in 1817, as an additional County Gaol because the one at Chester had become overcrowded. It had a surgeon, Chaplain, Schoolmaster and Schoolmistress. The prison was run by a Committee of magistrates, who met once a month, to deal with any business. Glazing the prison windows was discussed in 1842. It would cost £182 to glaze the windows of the cells, which at that time had shutters over them. The gaol was enlarged several times and could hold a maximum of 700.

From the Countryman's Ramble,

'The first thing we saw at the top of the town,
Was a building so grand, so high in renown,
That a Lord might live there, but one hardly believes,
That such a fine place, was built only for thieves.'

The gaol ceased to take criminals before the 1914 war. After the war had ended it was used by the Rev. Tubby Clayton (founder of Toc H), as an Ordination Test School, until 1922, when the few students left, were accommodated at Kilrie. The gaol was demolished in the mid 1930s.

(Below)
The staff lined up at Knutsford station in 1912, we presume they were photographed to celebrate the station's 50 years of operation. No wonder the service was good in those days!

(Inset)
Engine Shed at Knutsford Station about 1887. In the background can be seen the new tower of St. Cross Church (finished for the Jubilee Year). It is interesting to note the engine shed on the right, beyond the platform. Before the railway line was extended to Northwich, there was a shed here, where the engine was kept overnight. Note the carriages waiting for their owners to alight from the Manchester train. On the left-hand side, the coal sidings are level with the platform.

(Left)

This is a drawing by Richard Harding Watt. It is a copy of the original water colour painted by Anna Brandreth in 1846, when she painted her friend, Miss Lucy Holland, as the milkmaid. It is a view looking up King Street from the foot of Adam's Hill. Anna Brandreth was a most gifted amateur watercolour artist. She was sister-in-law to the Rev. Henry Green, the Unitarian Minister who wrote 'Knutsford – Its Traditions and History'. Another of her sisters, Jane, had married John Long whose family had been tanners in Knutsford for generations. Anna Brandreth lived with her parents in the third part of Heathfield House. The Brandreth family moved to Knutsford from Bolton in Lancashire.

(Above)

This is the prize-winning garden of Knutsford Station in 1933. It was the second time the staff had won first prize for the best garden on the Cheshire Lines Railway. The credit for such a magnificent display of colour, was due to the care and many hours of hard work put in by the late Mr. Bailey. What a pity the lawn and flower beds had to give way to parking space for the motor car, and what a loss to daily travellers on the line.

(Left)

An early photograph, (pre 1860) showing the bottom of Adam's Hill, and the old farm in King Street where Tommy Witter, a local poet and wit, had a weaving shed. These buildings were pulled down, to make way for the railway. Note the lamp standard, which was one of five in Knutsford – the last remaining one, now stands outside Tatton Park. These five lamp standards were erected in 1844 by the Freeholders, but it was forty years after their erection, that they finally brightened the darkness of Knutsford, with their gas light.

(Right)

A photograph of King Street taken about 1860 before the railway came to Knutsford. The row of brick cottages on the left of the photo, was pulled down to make way for the rail bridge over King Street, and the entrance to the Goods Yard. The first sod for the railway, was cut in 1860, and Knutsford had a new railway and a piped water supply in 1862.

(Below)

These timber framed cottages have always been known as the 'Tudor Cottages'. They were re-roofed with wooden shingles, after the thatch caught fire about 1940.

Whilst Deeds exist for these cottages from the 1780s, the cottages are older than the Deeds. Dr. Peter Holland (Mrs. Gaskell's uncle) owned the property in 1797, together with a Cheshire Acre of land, known as the Tentry Croft, behind them. A previous tenant had been James Boulton, a dyer, and father-in-law to Thomas Stringer, a Knutsford artist.

(Above)
Old cottage property in Swinton Square, off King Street. In 1760, the Rev. Robert Lord bought property on this street. He was a threadmaker, dealer and chapman, who was unable to mix business with religion (he was minister at Brook Street Chapel). He borrowed money – varying from small to large sums, from at least 63 people; but this did not help – he got deeper and deeper into debt. Finally he was declared bankrupt, and Peter Swinton administered his property to pay off the creditors. In 1802 when it was bought by the trustees of the late Samuel Egerton it was called 'Swinton's Square' an acknowledgement of Peter Swinton's work over the past thirty years.

Also in the square was the first Independent Chapel, which was replaced in 1865, by the Congregational Church on Brook Street.

(Above left)
An early photograph of Mrs. Betty Webster and neighbours. Many women took in washing – note the large water butts – very necessary for their trade, when these houses had no other water supply. The cottages must have always been very damp, with so much washing constantly drying. Mrs. Webster was also noted for the humbugs she made and sold. Her cottage, and the ones adjacent, have been replaced by houses Nos. 1–13 King Street.

(Left)
Gidmans shop decorated for the May Day celebrations. The banner over the two shops reads 'Tis a Glorious thing I ween. To be a Royal May Queen'. Nellie Gidman was the May Queen in the year 1892. The baby in the arms of her mother, was May Queen in 1906.

(Left) Gidmans workmen in 1890.

(Below left)

Gidman's Basketware shop was in King Street. The workmen are behind the shop making baskets from the willows which were brought from Ashley, and had to be boiled and stripped before they could be used. A Trade Directory lists the proprietor as John Gidman, cooper, prize churn and dairy utensil manufacturer, brush, basket and toy dealer.

(Below)

Sylvia Gidman, May Queen in 1906.

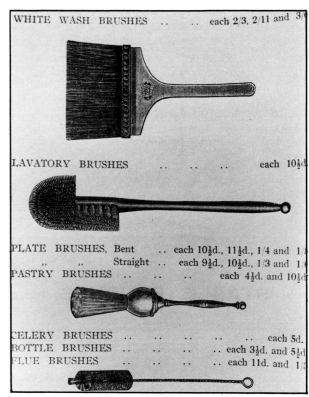

(Inset)
William Watson founded his high-class grocery business in 1852, and it flourished until quite recently. The aroma of freshly baked bread and roasting coffee is remembered by older residents, as is the service which Watson's provided:– tea blended to customers taste from Japanned canisters, biscuits mixed from many boxes, bacon sliced to required thickness, and a chair to sit on while your order was taken. It would then be delivered to your door. In earlier days they supplied their customers with an annual catalogue/price list which not only included wines and spirits, but ranged from food to candles, brushes to patent medicines.

(Left)
Staff photographed outside Watsons shop in 1913.

(Below Left)
Horse-drawn delivery vans drawn up under the Parish church wall, at the start of the day.

WHITE WASH BRUSHES	.. ..	each 2/3, 2/11 and 3/
LAVATORY BRUSHES	.. .. ..	each 10½d.
PLATE BRUSHES, Bent	..	each 10½d., 11½d., 1/4 and 1/
„ „ Straight	..	each 9½d., 10½d., 1/3 and 1/
PASTRY BRUSHES	.. .. ..	each 4½d. and 10½d.
CELERY BRUSHES	.. ..	each 5d.
BOTTLE BRUSHES	.. .. ..	each 3½d. and 5½d.
FLUE BRUSHES	.. .. ..	each 11d. and 1/

A page from Watson's Catalogue, 1913.

(Above)
One of the older properties in Knutsford. The thatched roofs have been replaced, and the simple shops shown in this photo, including Hannah Lowe's tiny shop, have been updated into an exclusive dress shop, La Boutique D'Or. It is quite possible that these premises existed in the mid 1600s.

(Right)
Miss Bailey standing outside her original shop, about 1920. Before she retired from her thriving fish and poultry shop, Miss Bailey had enlarged it to a double fronted shop which also sold greengroceries. It is now the delicatessen shop on King Street.

FISH, FRU
AND
GAME DEAL

(Inset)

Old Druncon Scarbrow, Hat and Feather, 1790. We would love to know which Knutsford resident 'earned' this nickname, which survives to this day, stamped on his jug. We also wonder why, if he was always so inebriated, did his jug survive – perhaps the landlord poured the ale out for him.

(Above)

King Street before Watt's buildings were erected. Beyond the Rose and Crown Inn, was the Hat and Feather Inn. When the Hat and Feather was demolished 1907–8, Watt planned to build a Post Office here, a more central position, but withdrew his offer when the Council and townsfolk seemed indifferent. Instead, he extended the Memorial Tower building to make the Kings Coffee House, a socially inspired concept to provide a meeting place, library, and concert room.

18

The Gaskell Memorial Tower, built by Richard Harding Watt in 1907, became the focal point of King Street. It is clear from the speech he made at the inaugural ceremony that Watt had faced some opposition. He said that he hoped the people of Knutsford would 'forget and forgive' and accept his building as a 'token of their mutual regard' for Mrs. Gaskell. He added that he found the 'best and most unanimous committee was a committee of one' (i.e. himself). His works in Knutsford stand as testimony to his individuality.

The original Cross Keys was shown as Egerton property in 1786, but it was built earlier than this. In 1841, Hannah Borrow aged 30 was the innkeeper with her sisters Jane, aged 23 and Ann aged 20 helping her. Quite an undertaking for three young ladies.

John Gledhill the licensee in the 1860s advertised in Morris's 1864 Directory:

Cross Keys Inn,
King Street,
Knutsford.

Licensed to let horses and carriages for hire.
Every Accommodation for travellers.
Good stabling and loosebox.
Well-aired beds.
An Omnibus to Chelford Daily and to Macclesfield every Thursday and Saturday.

This Cross Keys Inn was demolished in 1909, and when it was rebuilt, it was set back from the road, as we see it today.

An original drawing by Richard Harding Watt, showing the tower flanked by the old Cross Keys, the old Hat and Feather, and the old Rose and Crown inns.

(Above)

Mr. Fred Lee and family, Mr. Fred Lee was the owner of the old Hat and Feather Inn, which Richard Harding Watt demolished to make way for the Courtyard next to the newly built Gaskell Memorial Tower and Kings Coffee House. Whilst Fred Lee was the licensee of the Hat and Feather, he built a row of cottages on land which he owned behind (Church View). They were a 'peace offering' to his wife, when she discovered he was having yet another affair with yet another woman. These pretty cottages were built for £750. Fred Lee was the licensee of the White Lion Inn until he ended his life by hanging himself there. The Lee family also owned Austin Craven, Wine Merchants on Princess Street. Austin Craven's premises were partly demolished to make way for the present Co-op Supermarket.

The 1881 Census Returns lists Fred Lee as an ironmonger aged 17, living with his widowed mother who was a retired publican, and his brother George, who was 21, and was a horse dealer. The family at this time, were living in the Market Place. For many years, George Lee who was known as 'Crackers' Lee, led the May Day procession on his white horse.

(Above)

The Rose and Crown name refers to the Wars of the Roses, but the age of this inn is unknown. The date 1647 is visible on some old photographs but it is probable that there was an earlier Rose and Crown on the site. It has seen many changes over the years. At the time of this photograph (1861) it was not being used as an inn. (See also page 47.)

(Below)

The Wildgoose brothers, George and Frank, outside their shop which was next to the Rose and Crown Inn on King Street.

The premises had originally been built in 1754, by Pool Hurst, part owner of the Silk Mill, which stood behind the house, in Silkmill Street.

In 1899 William Wildgoose & Sons advertised themselves as 'General Drapers, Ladies & Gents Outfitters, Household Linens, Bedsteads & Bedding, Tailoring, Liveries Supplied, Funerals Furnished, Agent for Pullars & Sons, Dyers, of Perth'. At this time, the Wildgoose family did not own the premises next to their shop. These had been a doctor's residence for many years, and were then used as the Convervative Club.

George Wildgoose (Left)

(Above)

History is often out of sight! This fine plaster ceiling is upstairs in the Cheshire Building Society's offices in King Street. This ceiling appears to be the work of the craftsman who decorated a ceiling in Dukenfield Hall. This property, and the buildings on either side of it, are alleged to have been a dower house for the Leghs of Booths. Whilst the Leghs had property on the East side of King Street in 1641, it is not possible to identify this building from the list of owners and occupiers at that date.

This interesting old building with a weavers' gallery, was at one time a farm, with the outbuildings later used as a workshop. It was the property of the Hopes, who had a small shop when this photograph was taken in 1880. A tiny tea and refreshment room of S. Heyes is in part of the building.

This property was demolished by Henry Pemberton, and the District Bank then occupied its place. It is now an auctioneers and estate agents – Frank R. Marshall & Co.

A carved fireplace which existed in a bedroom in a premise in King Street. It has the Legh of Booths coat-of-arms above the fire opening. At one time the Leghs of Booths owned 19 premises in King Street.

(Right)
Some shops never change! Titus Lees, ironmonger, King Street, with a display of his wares outside his shop. The shop today is still an ironmongers, known as Hitchmough's.

(Right)
This old photograph records an important stage in the hotel's history. The word 'Royal' was added to its name after the visit of Princess Victoria in 1832, five years before she became Queen.

The modern inn sign shows George II but the inn was licensed as 'The George and Dragon' and the sign still depicted this in 1848. The cornices of the archway in this photo are plain, but now they show old plasterwork decoration with St. George and the Dragon, probably revealed during alterations made about 1910.

Fourteenth century origins have been claimed for the inn, and it certainly existed in 1653 when Sir Thomas Mainwaring met his Parliamentary colleagues 'at the George about the Act of Creditors and Poore Prisoners'.

The George's hey-day came with the coaching era. It was patronised by the gentry who built the Assembly Rooms by raising subscriptions. The Assemblies held in the winter months, financed the race meetings held on the Heath.

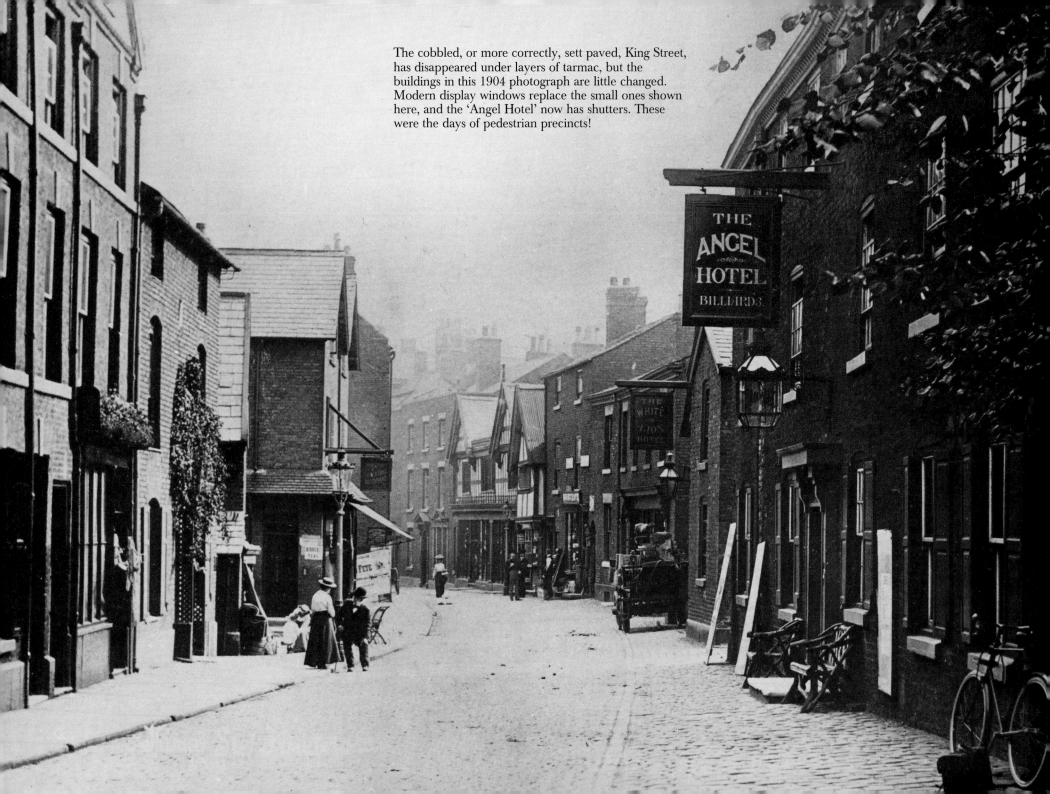

The cobbled, or more correctly, sett paved, King Street, has disappeared under layers of tarmac, but the buildings in this 1904 photograph are little changed. Modern display windows replace the small ones shown here, and the 'Angel Hotel' now has shutters. These were the days of pedestrian precincts!

The post office in this photograph was built in 1894 by Mr. Thrutchley and leased to the G.P.O.

Richard Harding Watt made alterations to the building when he initiated the Cranford Club on the first floor. Above the clock is a bas relief sculpture of Mrs. Gaskell. Watt later removed it, and set it into the side of the Gaskell Memorial Tower, where it can still be seen today.

Knutsford has had a post office since the mid-1600s, when Jeffery Aldcroft combined the duties of postmaster, with that of innkeeper of the Rose & Crown.

During the 1800s. various premises on top and bottom streets were used for post office business.

(Right)

The northern end of King Street did not always end with the wooded area which is there today. When Humphrey Repton prepared his landscaping schemes for William Egerton of Tatton, one of his sketches showed the 'miserable cottages' which went right up to the entrance to the park. These were 'bought up' and then demolished, so that they did not detract from the imposing entrance designed by Repton.

The large house on the right, was built about 1700, by Henry Antrobus, a wealthy C17 mercer, whose charitable bequest to the town helped apprentices in the past, and still provides educational grants to students. He also left money to the 'preaching minister' of Knutsford and the schoolmaster. The house was drawn by Humphrey Repton in 1791. When he sketched it, it had three windows on the first and second floors, as it has today. This photo shows only two windows on each floor, presumably the centre two were bricked up to avoid paying the window tax.

(Left)

The Old Vicarage, King Street. This house, now the last one on the east side of King Street, was one of six houses built by Henry Antrobus, a wealthy Knutsford mercer. When he died in 1713, he left all his property to his sole surviving sister, Margaret Furnes. She died three years later, and left this house 'in perpetuity to the episcopally ordained preaching minister of Knutsford'. Many of the ministers preferred to live elsewhere, and the premises were rented out. At one time it was a boarding school for boys.

Mrs. Gaskell had this house in mind when she wrote the scene in Cranford about Peter, the Vicar's son.

It was in a very run-down state, when rescued, and given a new lease of life by the present owners, Stuart Hague & Company.

(Below Right & Left)

Watt's Eastern style laundry complex was built on the site of a tannery in Drury Lane, in the early years of this century. Its minarets, domes and towers created a fantastic skyline but not a very practical laundry. The green tiled tower bore the words 'Let thy garments be always white'. It is believed that the tower was Watt's adaptation of a similar building which he saw in Damascus.

(Left)
Rowley's Ironmongery and Pot Shop. The later photograph shows the shop after the thatched roof caught fire.

(Below)
Rowley's Ironmongery and Pot Shop was demolished after the thatched roof caught fire in the 1960s. Knutsford lost a building which had stood at the top of the Market Place for centuries, and which was architecturally unique in Cheshire.

(Above Top)
The horse-drawn laundry vans assembled in King Street.

(Above)
Richard Harding Watt built the Recreation Rooms on Drury Lane for his laundry workers, pictured here about 1910. He greatly admired Ruskin, and incorporated extracts from his works carved on stone panels, a feature which can be found on other Watt's buildings. Part of the Ruskin Rooms was at one time used as a fire station. The building now contains offices and the British Legion meeting rooms.

(Right)

The silk Mill which gave its name to this street was built in 1754. It did not flourish, probably due to difficulties of supply and demand; cotton was also spun here, before the Egertons bought the bankrupt mill, and converted it to houses in 1818.

Census returns show a very large population lived in small houses such as these. In the 1851 census, one house had '41 Irish travelling north, slept on the floor overnight'.

(Below)

The Old Court House in the Market Place, and the once fashionable houses built in the 1740s and known as Argyle Court. The Old Court House was used by the Egertons to hold their Courts Leet and Courts Barron from the early 1700s. Performing bears entertained outside, whilst meat and dairy products were sold under cover inside.

For centuries this was the hub for market trade in Knutsford. The upper floor of the Court House was used as an armoury during the Napoleonic wars, and it was in this room that the Rev. Green delivered his lectures 'Knutsford – Its Traditions and History', and later published as a book.

The Silk Mill Street cinema, known latterly as the Old Picture House, was built in the days of silent films, with background music provided by a pianist. The indoor market now occupies the site. The earliest filmshows were put on by Captain Payne, in a tent in Brook Street – umbrellas were needed on wet days!

The power for his projector was generated by a steam engine, and the town crier advertised the forthcoming programme.

(Right)

The Parochial School for Boys at the bottom of Adam's Hill. This small building was supposed to accommodate 200. There was no play area except the roadway in front of the school. The school was built before 1830, on land given by the Egerton family. It was maintained by the Parish rate, subscriptions and fees. Many times Levi Todd wrote in his log book 'sent several boys home for their school pence', until, on June 14th, 1903, when he wrote 'Received notice from Cheshire County Education Committee that after 30th June, school pence will cease to be charged'.

Ethel Todd, the May Queen in 1907 (Below).

(Left)

The Todd family were, for many years, the mainstay of Knutsford's education. Levi Todd was headmaster of the boys' Parochial School at the bottom of Adam's Hill, and later, the new Egerton Boys' School opposite the Parish Church. His period of service at both schools covered 44 years, from 1876–1920. Known to the boys as 'Gaffer' Todd, he also sang in the church choir, was a prominent freemason, and a founder member of the town's cricket club. It is surprising that he had time for leisure, because in the 1880s the school day began at 7am, with lessons for the pupil teachers, and ended, with night school in the evening.

Mrs. Todd was headmistress of the Infant School in Silk Mill Street. The Todd's youngest daughter, Ethel, was the May Queen in 1907.

(Above Left)
Form IV Boys at Egerton School about 1906.

(Above Right)
Schoolchildren at Crosstown school photographed in 1920. Crosstown school was situated on the Mobberley Road opposite St. Cross church and graveyard. It was a National School built in 1860.

Joseph and Mary Magee were Master and Mistress in 1874. In 1892 the average attendance was 200. Many Knutsfordians received their early education here until a few years ago, when a new, larger school was built to replace it. The school has recently been demolished, and mews style houses now occupy the site of the school and playground.

(Left)
Pupils and staff in front of Henry Newland's School. Henry Newland's School on Manchester Road dates from about 1860. He took in a limited number of boarders, and a few select day pupils. He advertised his school in Morris's Directory for Cheshire, and the Macclesfield Courier.

The curriculum included Reading, Writing, Spelling, Arithmetic, Mensuration and Land Surveying, Mechanics, Algebra, Geometry, Book-keeping, Geography, Map Drawing, Grammar, Composition and English History.

French and German, Drawing, Dancing, Drill and Music were also available on the terms of the respective masters. His pupils came from the nearby cotton towns, and further afield, including one boy who was 'born on the sea'.

(Below)

Knutsford had a Grammar School as early as Edward VI's reign. Sir John Legh of Booths was granted land in Knutsford, Sudlow (now only remembered as a 'lane') and Tabley, after the Dissolution of the Monasteries, provided that he and 'his heirs would from time to time for ever find one able schoolmaster, well and sufficiently learned for the teaching and bringing up of youth'.

John Legh agreed to pay a salary of £5-6-8d per annum, and continued to appoint the schoolmaster until the 1800s, by which time he was better paid.

To augment the salary of the schoolmaster in those early days, several wealthy Knutsford residents left money to him. William Allen, a blacksmith from Bexton, left £20 in 1682 to educate 6 poor children at the Grammar School until they could read well the Bible. Education at the early Grammar School was of a high standard. Latin would be expected to be taught.

In 1743 a new Grammar School was built on King Street, on the site of the Chapel of Ease. This school flourished for nearly 150 years until replaced by the third and last school. This picture shows the last Grammar School built in 1887, near the Heath, to house 25 boarders and 50 day boys. A Directory of about 1880 quotes terms for boarders at £35 per annum, and day pupils at £5 per annum. Financial problems caused it to close.

(Above)

The oldest building in Knutsford still used for worship. This protestant dissenters chapel dates from 1689, when the Act of Toleration granting freedom of worship, was passed. Its whitewashed walls and latticed windows create an air of serenity to all who visit it.

Mrs. Gaskell was a member of the congregation as a girl, and taught in the Sunday School. Mr. Benson's Chapel in 'Ruth' is drawn from her knowledge of Brook Street Chapel. Mrs. Gaskell is buried in the graveyard of the chapel, together with her husband and two unmarried daughters.

The Rev. George Payne and family were photographed by her grave. Students of Mrs. Gaskell's life and works, are indebted to the Rev. Payne for his book on Mrs. Gaskell. The Rev. Payne, as well as being Unitarian Minister for 40 years, was also the first honorary librarian when Knutsford's new library was opened in 1904.

From Medieval days, Knutsford had two chapels, one on King Street, and the other, known as the Parochial Chapel, situated a mile away across the fields, near Booths Hall. These were 'daughter' chapels to the 'Mother' church of Rostherne.

In 1741, an Act of Parliament was passed making Knutsford into a separate Parish. The two old chapels were demolished, and the new Parish Church was built on the 'Tentry Croft'. When the new church was built, the pews were sold to the parishioners in order to provide money to finish the church, and to enclose the churchyard.

Over the years, as Knutsford's population grew, the irritation of the poor at not being allowed to sit in these 'owned pews', increased.

With the help of Lance Bentley, a barrister living in Knutsford, who took up the fight on behalf of the working class in 1875, it was agreed (not without a struggle) to abolish 'owned pews'. This was helped by the discovery of dry rot in the existing pews.

In 1879, the large room over the Market Hall was licensed for Divine Service, whilst the Parish Church was re-pewed, and two vestries added.

When the church re-opened there was a notice on display stating 'all seats in this church are free'.

Church House (now known as Hollingford House) was the home of the Holland family. Dr. Peter Holland, Mrs. Gaskell's uncle, who lived here, was the model for several doctor characters in her novels (e.g. Mr. Hoggins – 'Cranford', Dr. Gibson – 'Wives and Daughters').

Mary and Lucy Holland, his daughters, each founded and financed their own infant schools in the town(Inset). The Directory for Cheshire gives us a description of the two schools.

'A neat infants' school and residence for the teacher was built around 1842, by Miss Lucy Holland. 65 children now attend the school.' Maria Drinkwater was the schoolmistress, and her husband was a farrier. The school, house, and blacksmith's forge were next to the Lord Eldon in Tatton Street (now replaced by Edmondson Electrical).

About the same time, Miss Mary Holland had a free school for infants in Silkmill Street. Maria Toft was the mistress in 1850. In 1860 the school moved to the last premise in Princess Street before Church Hill.

(Right)

The 1st St. Cross Church was designed and built by Peter Legh of Booths Hall, using a workforce and material from his estate. It was to replace the old church of St. Helena which was pulled down in 1741. This new church was consecrated on 13th February, 1858.

The church and Crosstown both took their name from the existence of an old stone cross, part of which, is preserved in the present church.

The boys in this photograph were from the boarding school run by the Vicar, the Rev. L. W. Riley, who before his appointment, had been master of the Grammar School in King Street.

The farmhouse next to the church was adapted to form the vicarage, and had also to accommodate the boarders from the Grammar School who came with the Rev. Riley on his appointment as Vicar. The stables became the schoolroom, and the floor above became the dormitories for the boys. At one time there were 35 people living in the Vicarage.

(Inset)

The Rev. L. W. Riley, M.A., was appointed Vicar of the new St. Cross church. He was vicar from 1858–1875.

(Left)

Old cottages on the Mobberley Road, which were demolished by George Acton in 1910. His son still lives in one of the houses which George built to replace them. George Acton was a builder by trade, and was responsible for the new cemetery in Knutsford. The stone for the wall surrounding the cemetery, came from a quarry near Runcorn, and the horse-drawn carts took several days to bring the stone to Knutsford. There have been Actons living in Knutsford since the 1500s. On the left is the now demolished Crosstown school.

(Left)
Junction of Brook Street and Hollow Lane, showing the Congregational church, and part of the old cottage which had a beam dated 1411, but more likely to be 1711

(Inset)
This old cottage was reputed to be the oldest building in Knutsford, before it was demolished. The beam taken from it is kept in the library. We believe the cottage was not as old as claimed.

(Below left)
Old cottages on the Mobberley Road. The steps up to the first one can still be seen. These were some of the properties which were overcrowded and had insufficient water supply, in the Report on the Housing of the Working Classes Committee in 1899. 584 houses in different parts of Knutsford were inspected. 76 were without any sanitary conveniences, 86 houses were without tap and slopstone, and 201 were without a proper water supply. These 201 houses, housed 871 persons – no wonder that there was an outbreak of cholera in Over Knutsford in the mid 1800s!

The Report also reveals the dilapidated state of some of the cottages. 'Leaking roofs, loose floor-flags, unflagged yards, as well as the absence of sanitary conveniences and independent water supply already mentioned, occur too frequently. Some occupiers admit that they endure discomforts and put up with sanitary defects in silence, rather than run the risk of being turned-out.'

The Report continues . . . 'that squalor should be associated with a town in a situation such as Knutsford boasts – surrounded by noble parks – indicates some abnormal condition in its municipal life which is certainly a reflection on all concerned'.

The chairman of the Committee was Richard Harding Watt, who at the same time, was building his Italian style houses for the better-off Knutsfordians.

Also in the photograph is the shop known as the 'County Stores', which was later extended. Its plasterwork motifs have recently been renovated.

Chelford Road looking towards the Legh Arms, and
Brook Street. There is no spire of the Congregational
Church in this photograph, so it is pre-1865. The black
and white cottage by the Legh Arms has long since
been demolished. The cottage stood alongside the lane
which was widened later, and which we know today as
Legh Road.

(Left)

The Watt's houses on Legh Road. Trees now obscure this view. Sir Nikolaus Pevsner in his 'Buildings of Cheshire' calls it the 'maddest sequence of villas in all England'. Here, Watt allowed free rein to his architectural designs, while wealthy Manchester businessmen payed for his unique creations.

(Below Left)

Old cottages on the Chelford Road (now demolished), looking towards the Legh Arms and Brook Street. The spire of the Congregational Church is also on the photograph.

The Congregational Church was built in 1865 at a cost of £5,000. The steeple had to be removed when it was discovered that the ground the church was built on, was unstable. The church was sold in 1937, and was finally demolished in the 1940s.

(Below Right)

These cottages known as 'Pump Cottages', are still standing on the Chelford Road, but have been very much 'improved' since this photograph was taken. One of them was a beerhouse called the 'Ring O' Bells'.

An inventory of a wheelwright, Thomas Wright, who died in 1733, lists his brewing house and equipment – he would have combined his work as a wright, with serving refreshments to thirsty travellers. Thomas Wright lived in one of these cottages.

Grange Cottage, Chelford Road. This is one of Knutsford's older buildings. The rendered exterior gives no clues to the wealth of beams which have been exposed in the interior of the house. Originally this would have been an open hall, single storey building. In the course of its life, an upper floor and staircase have been added.

It is probable that Richard Bertington was the occupant of this house in 1641. In 1850 it was a Dame School, where, it is alleged, the school marm could not read or write. This was probably Jane Roylance, who gave her occupation as 'Schoolmistress' when the census enumerator called, in 1841.

The Courthouse, Over Knutsford. When this building was built, this part of Knutsford was known as Over Knutsford, Higher Knutsford, or Knutsford Superior. This was the Courthouse with cells underneath, where justice was meted out to wrongdoers, and local matters were settled by the Squire and his jurymen.

By the time this photograph was taken, it was rented by the Rev. Clowes, and it no longer housed the lawbreakers in its cells. The ladies in the crinolines are the Misses Clowes, the daughters of the Vicar. They were instrumental in the founding of the May Day ceremony in Knutsford.

(Above Left and Right)

Booths Mill. A Corn mill has stood by the side of the
Birkin Brook, on the Mobberley, Knutsford boundary,
since Medieval days. The earlier mills relied entirely on
water for their power. The mill pool was leased in 1862
to provide a piped water supply to Knutsford. As
Knutsford grew in population, the pressure was
insufficient, and, just over 100 years ago, the water
tower on the Mobberley road was built to improve the
supply.

After torrential rain in 1946, the side of the mill pool
was breached, and the water drained away. The mill
was still grinding corn until it was sold to Macclesfield
Farmers in 1957.

(Left)

The hunt meeting outside Booths Hall. This is the new
hall built in 1745, and enlarged in 1845. The old hall
was the home of the Legh family for centuries. It stood
on clay ground, surrounded by a moat.

The Leghs raised soldiers in Over and Nether
Knutsford to go with them to fight for the King.
Knutsford men fought alongside their squire at Crecy,
Rheims and Poitiers.

Meet of the Cheshire Hounds. Booth Hall, Knutsford

Thorneyholme, a large mock Tudor house, was built c.1890 by Charles Galloway, who made his fortune as an engineer and boiler maker. His small daughter laid the foundation stone to the house. One of his sons later used to refer to the house as 'Biler Hall'. This son, killed in the Boer War, is remembered in the stained glass West Window of St. Cross Church. Mr. Galloway also donated the window on the South side of the church, in memory of his wife. These two windows were from the firm of Morris & Co., from designs by Sir Edward Burne-Jones.

Charles Galloway superintended the building of the Furness Railway Viaduct across Ulverstone sands. He was awarded the Legion of Honour for his work at the Paris exhibitions of 1879 and 1889. He was a patron of the Arts, and a magistrate for 30 years.

Two lodges of 'Thorneyholme' remain. The house became derelict after war-time occupation by U.S. troops, and had to be demolished in the early 1950s.

Grove House once stood in all its grandeur surrounded by flower beds and well kept lawns. It appears in the Land Tax Assessment of 1799. Mrs. Martha Antrobus. Grove House, Buildings and Gardens. The Tax paid on it was 14/9d.

The style of its architecture in the photograph is late Regency, which suggests it was 'improved' after it was built. Mrs. Antrobus only enjoyed the new house for a few years. By 1810 she was dead, and it was owned by Captain (later Major) Irvine, and it was rented out to respectable families. Sir Jeremiah Dixon lived at Grove House in 1828. Maria Banks, Lydia Brook and Adelaide Dixon, three ladies of Independent means, lived at Grove House in 1841, with their 10 servants. Mrs. Emma Tatton was a tenant there in 1850. Mr. John Long of the tanning family, lived there for many years in the late 1800s, and Mr. George Holt with his family came to live at Grove House in 1907.

The reminiscences of the late Mr. Wood, which were written down in 1940, recalls that John Wood who lived in Knutsford from 1730–1809, made the imposing wrought iron gates at the entrance to Grove House, and that these gates were still there on October 13th, 1940.

After the house was demolished, an estate of small houses was built in the 1950s in the grounds of the grand house.

The Honble. Mrs Jamieson's mentioned in "Cranford"

Brook House. The original house was built by Isaac Antrobus, a wealthy Knutsford skinner, who gave part of his land for the building of the Dissenter's Chapel in the late 1680s.

Over the years, Brook House was extended, and different families lived in it. One of its tenants was Lady Jane Stanley, who is alleged to have sent her footman out to stop the coaches as they approached the town, in order that she might learn the latest news and gossip before her fellow townsfolk! The sedan chair she used for visiting, is still to be seen each year in our Royal May Day procession.

Louisa Carbutt had a very successful girls' boarding school in Brook House in the 1860s. She was a very enlightened teacher for her day.

James and Frances Eastwood took over her school in the 1870s. Holford Crescent flats and houses now occupy the site of Brook House and its large garden.

Racing on Knutsford Heath was the sport of gentlemen who came from Lancashire and Cheshire to race their horses as early as the mid-1600s. The races were later financed from the Assemblies held at the 'George'.

The grandstand in this photograph, replacing an earlier one, was built in 1865 by a company formed to make the racing profitable, but their enterprise failed, and racing finished in 1873.

'Sandilands', near the Heath, is reputed to have been built using the bricks, stone, and timber from the dismantled grandstand.

THE GRAND STAND, KNUTSFORD.

(Above Left)
This group of girls from St. Cross School, entertained the convalescent soldiers during the 1st World War, at 'Thrutchley's Palace', now known as 'Kilrie'.

(Above Right)
A photograph showing 'Heath Grange', later to be known as 'Thrutchley's Palace' after the name of the family who lived in it, and, later, as 'Kilrie'. Note the young lime trees planted at the turn of the century, with funds from the Freeholders, and Lady Jane Stanley's charity.

(Right)
Reuben Pearson was one of Knutsford's 'characters', still remembered for his eccentricities. His home on Manchester Road, shown here, became a 'health hydro' where his patients found relief from pain with his skilful massage treatments.

When Miss Vera Rivaz wrote her 'Talking of Knutsford' memories she described Reuben Pearson as 'a little stout man with a merry smile and magic in his fingers'. During the 1st World War he used to visit the Red Cross Hospital (now Kilrie) to treat the soldiers. His jokes were of the type the nurses pretended to turn a deaf ear to, but the soldiers, of course, loved them, and his morning in the wards was the bright spot of the day for them.

(Below)

The old fire station showing one of the horse-drawn fire engines with its crew. The fire station (originally a Blacksmiths shop) was situated on the Northwich Road, near to the night asylum (doss house). For emergencies the key was kept at George Lees. George lived next to what is now the Tatton Club, in Tatton Street.

(Bottom)

Heathside Cafe, and some of the cottages which made up Gannon Square. The artisans living in these cottages in 1881, included tinsmiths, blacksmiths, wheelwrights, bricklayers, gardeners, and farm labourers. Eighteen families lived in the tiny cottages which made up the square. In the background is the new bypass, King Edward Road, which was opened in 1937.

(Above)

Trumpet Major Smith who sounded the charge at Balaclava, and who served in India during the mutiny. He was decorated with six medals and eight clasps, representing 14 engagements. In 1863 he was Trumpet Major to the Earl of Chester's Yeomanry, retiring in 1874 after 35 years continuous service.

He then became manager of the Gentleman's Club in Tatton Street, the Town Crier, and also the Court Crier at the Quarter Sessions at Chester and Knutsford. He was greatly missed after his tragic death through taking too much laudanum with too much alcohol. He lived latterly in the last house in Freeholders Terrace, Love Lane (now Stanley Road).

The House of Mrs Lumb where
Mrs Gaskell lived from age of 2 to 13

Elizabeth Stevenson (later to marry the Rev. Gaskell) was brought to this house of her aunt, Mrs. Lumb, as a baby, and lived here happily until she went away to a boarding school near Stratford-on-Avon.

Samuel Wright, a Knutsford attorney, lived in this house, known as Thorleys, before Mrs. Lumb rented it. In 1789, he planted one Newington peach tree, and one nectarine, the two trees costing 3/-, two dwarf greengage trees 2/-, one morello cherry tree 2/-, and two moss roses 3/- which he purchased from the nursery of William Caldwell, together with a collection of vegetable seeds.

To Samuel Wright fell the major task of preparing for, and building, the new Parish Church of St. John the Baptist in the early 1740s.

(Right)

Heathfield House. This is reputed to be the home of Edward Higgins, Knutsford's notorious highwayman, who was executed at Carmarthen in 1767. From 1741, it was known as the Cann Office, the place where weights and measures were checked, and to the locals as the 'Cannie House' due to the alleged secret passages through which Higgins was supposed to have escaped from the constables.

The Land Tax Assessments of 1791, show that a Colonel Handfield resided here, and that it was his newly built residence, so Edward Higgins could never have lived in the house which is here today.

Prior to 1789, there were three smaller houses on the site. Higgins lived in one of these. He had married into the Bertles family, and this property belonged to the Bertles, as did another large house, at the north end of King Street. By 1841, the house had reverted to three separate premises, but became one again when Robert Earl had his boarding school in the house, and the Merriman family lived in it in 1881.

(Left)
1887 was the year of Queen Victoria's Golden Jubilee. The Prince and Princess of Wales were visiting Manchester to open a 'Jubilee' Exhibition at the White City. It had also been planned that the Prince would cut the first sod of the Manchester Ship Canal, but by May, insufficient money had been raised, so the ceremony was postponed until later on in the year, when Lord Egerton, who was Chairman of the Company, cut the first sod with the silver-plated spade which is now on display at Tatton Hall.

On May 2nd the Prince and Princess, left Euston Station at 2pm, and after changing trains at Crewe, they went via Sandbach, Middlewich and Northwich, arriving at Knutsford a few minutes before 6pm. A Guard-of-Honour, formed by the 3rd Cheshire Volunteers, and the Cheshire Yeomanry, lined Adam's Hill as the carriage, drawn by four bay horses, made its way up King Street to Tatton Park, where the Prince and Princess stayed overnight as guests of Lord and Lady Egerton. A reporter described the decorations and sanding in King Street as 'one continued arabesque'.

Next day, May 3rd, on their way to open the Manchester Exhibition, the 'Macclesfield Courier' reported 'Their Royal Highnesses witnessed a rehearsal of crowning the May Queen and as a sign of their appreciation, the Prince authorised the Chairman of the Committee to style it 'Royal' in days to come'.

This rehearsal, with Mary Howarth as the May Queen, sitting on her throne surrounded by her retinue, took place outside the Town Hall.

The full May Day celebrations were held later on the Heath on 19th May, which was Queen Victoria's birthday.

(Far Left)
Mary Howarth, the 1st 'Royal' May Queen, 1887.

(Left)

The child riding in the sedan chair which had belonged to Lady Jane Stanley, is Ida Rose Jackson. Sticky Wright and Billy Bostock were the carriers. Five years later, in 1919, Ida Rose Jackson was the May Queen, riding in the greater comfort of the open carriage.

(Above)

Doris Pemberton, the Jubilee May Queen in 1914, photographed outside her parents shoe shop in King Street. This was the 50th year of the May Day celebrations in Knutsford, and, because of the War, this was the last May Day until 1919.

(Right and left)

The May Queen of 1881 was Mary Hickson, who was the daughter of William Hickson, saddler. The rag rug was brought out, and laid over the cobbles of the yard, when Mary was photographed with some of her retinue. Photographed at the same time, sitting on the May Queen's velvet cloak is a friend of the family, a Miss Stevenson, who was a dressmaker. Other friends who were also photographed include a Mrs. Paulden and a Mr. Nichols. The family lived at 93 King Street, and William had paid £600 for this property when it was auctioned at the George Hotel, on 17th September, 1877.

(Above Left)
Some of the members of the Ordination Test School taking part in the May Day procession of 1919. After the end of the 1st World War, many ex-soldiers wished to be ordained ministers. Knutsford gaol was used to accommodate and train them, and it was known as the Ordination Test School. It was directed by Rev. Tubby Clayton, founder of Toc H.

(Above Right)
Morris Dancers outside the Old Town Hall in 1902. They became part of the May Day celebrations after the new May Day Committee of 1878 invited the Godley Hill men's team from Hyde to take part. Other troupes were formed, including the Leyland troupe in 1889. Knutsford May Day played a part in reviving interest in Morris Dancing.

(Left)
Knutsford as it might have been. In 1901 there were complaints that the Post Office at the far end of King Street was out of the way for many people. Watt submitted this design for a new Post Office to be built between the Memorial Tower and the Rose and Crown Inn. He withdrew his offer, annoyed by the indifference of the Council, and instead, used the pillars from St. Peter's Church, Manchester, as part of the Coffee House Courtyard.

The Rose and Crown about 1906.

Mrs. Gaskell's happy childhood in Knutsford provided her with a store of material which she was to draw on when she wrote 'Cranford', 'Wives and Daughters', 'Mr. Harrison's Confessions' and 'The Squire's Story'. Her affection for Knutsford has ensured that our small, friendly town is known the world over.